Learning in Early Years

Enhancing Provision Through

Superheroes

Ideas to Target Learning and Challenge Thinking

Nicky Simmons & Ginny Morris

Enhancing Provision Through Superheroes

First Edition: May 2017

@2017 Nicky Simmons & Ginny Morris
All rights reserved

ISBN: 1546698302
ISBN-13: 978-1546698302

About The Authors

Ginny Morris

Ginny has a wide range of experience teaching Early Years in both mainstream and special school settings.

She was the leader of a highly successful Foundation Unit for seven years, during which time she also supported and mentored other Early Years settings within the Local Authority.

Nicky Simmons

Nicky was a Primary School Head Teacher for ten years. During her headship she provided a strategic vision for the school, transforming it into a dynamic learning environment.

She was known for her charismatic style and solution focused approach.

We now run Morris & Simmons Education, a training and consultancy company. We write and deliver a wide program of professional development packages and produce our own books and resources for Early Years practitioners.

As well as creating and delivering our own training programmes, we also regularly work with different settings on Consultancy and Improvement Projects. We offer simple solutions, model good practice and coach practitioners to help them improve their practice and provision. Our Provision Makeovers are proving particular popular.

We feel very privileged to be able to share our knowledge, experience and expertise with talented and creative practitioners, who continue to challenge our thinking and present us with new and exciting opportunities. For more information about our work visit our website www.morrissimmons.com or email mse@morrissimmons.com.

Acknowledgements

Throughout our careers we have been privileged to work with so many talented colleagues, children and families, many of whom have significantly contributed to our expertise. We are very grateful for their challenge, inspiration and belief in our abilities, always pushing us to reach new heights.

We are also very grateful to all the amazing practitioners that we have met since starting Morris & Simmons Education. Thank you for inspiring us to seek new solutions by giving us different perspectives and sharing your own challenges and successes.

A very special thank you, for this publication, to Curdworth Primary School. We had a great time setting up the activities and working alongside and with the staff and children. We enjoyed watching and listening to how they tackled our Superhero challenges and your feedback was invaluable. Our favourite comment has to be from one little boy "I love them all!"

We are also very grateful for the support from Teachers' Time (www.teachertime.co.uk), a website providing practical teaching aids for Early Years practitioners. We really appreciate their permission to use some of their creative resources in our activities.

Finally we would like to thank our families without whose support, encouragement and technical expertise none of this work would have been possible.

How To Use This Book

Our 'Learning in Early Years' collection was written following our highly successful publication '**Planning for Learning in Early Years**'.

We had lots of requests asking for practical advice about how and what to provide in continuous provision in order to help children meet their next steps in learning and make accelerated progress. We observed that learning led by the adult was often well planned for and learning was explicit. However, the learning in continuous provision was often diluted and activities were simply 'nice to have'.

Our work supporting practitioners with planning their provision inspired us to write books that:

- Target learning by exemplifying "**I am learning to...**" statements
- Provide open-ended ideas
- Challenge children to think more deeply

Each book in the collection provides a selection of open-ended challenges, which can be delivered both indoors and outside and can be flexibly used as part of continuous provision. They are designed to give busy practitioners a good starting point for planning their provision.

Each challenge is laid out in an easy to use grid which helps all practitioners to know:

- How to resource and set up the challenge
- The specific learning each challenge could possibly target
- How maths and writing skills can be applied across areas of learning

We would strongly advise that you choose one area from the suggested focused learning possibilities section that is most appropriate for your children's next steps, so observations are focused and learning does not become diluted.

Each book in the collection is easy to use and intended to inspire both adults and children. Pick and choose the ideas; adapt, tweak, add to and extend them, so that they match your children's interests and challenge them to achieve their next steps in learning.

Enhancing Provision Through Superheroes

Contents

Areas of Learning: An Overview 1

Super Rescue 3

Super Mitts 5

Super Talk 7

Symmetrical Capes 9

Super Character 11

Super Tools 13

Super Shapes 15

Super Touch 17

Super Words 19

Measuring Sticks 21

Metal Man 23

Super Scene 25

Elastic Man 27

Super Strong 29

Baddie Traps 31

Exciting Explosions 33

Kryptonite Calculations 35

Super Sticky 37

Enhancing Provision Through Superheroes

Areas of Learning: An Overview

Area of Learning		Challenges
PSED	Making Relationships	Super Scene
	Self-Confidence & Self-Awareness	Super Touch, Kryptonite Calculations
	Managing Feelings & Behaviour	Super Words
Communication & Language	Listening & Attention	Super Mitts
	Understanding	Measuring Sticks, Kryptonite Calculations
	Speaking	Super Rescue, Super Talk, Symmetrical Capes, Super Shapes, Super Touch, Measuring Sticks, Metal Man, Super Scene, Baddie Traps, Exciting Explosions, Super Sticky
Physical Development	Moving & Handling	Super Mitts, Super Talk, Super Character, Super Tools, Super Shapes, Elastic Man, Super Strong, Super Sticky
	Health & Self-Care	
Literacy	Reading	Super Words, Exciting Explosions
	Writing	Super Talk, Super Tools, Super Words
Mathematics	Numbers	Super Mitts, Kryptonite Calculations
	Shape, Space & Measure	Super Rescue, Symmetrical Capes, Super Shapes, Measuring Sticks, Elastic Man
Understanding the World	People & Communities	
	The World	Super Touch, Metal Man, Super Strong, Exciting Explosions, Super Sticky
	Technology	Super Rescue
Expressive Arts & Design	Exploring & Using Media & Materials	Super Character, Metal Man, Super Strong, Symmetrical Capes
	Being Imaginative	Super Scene, Baddie Traps

Challenge: **Super Rescue** Suggested Area of Provision: **Outside**

Enhance with:	Invite your children to:	Other enhancements:
- A square grid made with masking tape - Arrows - Pictures of villains, superheroes and characters to rescue - Pictures of potential challenges e.g. fire, river, mountains, volcanoes, ice etc - Key vocabulary e.g. prepositional and directional words i.e. next to, beside, near, far, top, bottom, beside, before, after, direction, left, right, forwards, backwards, sideways, towards, between, middle, behind	Place the arrows on the grid to provide a route for a superhero to follow to rescue a character avoiding the villains and dangers.	- Add a list of instructions for children to follow so that they must visit certain squares in the right order before they can rescue the character - Add a programmable toy for children to send around the grid.

Select From the Following Suggested Focused Learning Possibilities

Communication & Language — Speaking	Mathematics — Shape, Space & Measure	Understanding the World — Technology
Use this challenge to: Provide opportunities for your children to narrate and describe their thinking as they tackle a problem.	**Use this challenge to:** Provide opportunities for your children to use and apply mathematical language.	**Use this challenge to:** Provide opportunities for your children to practise imputing information into programmable toys,
I am learning to... - talk in simple sentences (22-36) - explain what is happening (30-50) - talk about my ideas (40-60)	**I am learning to...** - use prepositional words (30-50) - use prepositions to describe where something is (40-60) - use the correct vocabulary to talk about position (ELG)	**I am learning to...** - operate simple toys (22-36) - operate toys to achieve a desired effect (30-50) - use a simple computer program (40-60)
Challenge your children to: Give reasons for their decisions and choices.	**Challenge your children to:** Add grid references to help them locate a specific square e.g. B3 has the Joker	

Characteristics of Effective Learning:

Engagement: I am learning about how making mistakes can help me with my learning
Motivation: I am learning to try different ways of doing things when one approach doesn't work
Thinking: I am learning to set hypotheses and test out my ideas

Mark Making/Writing Opportunities

Invite your children to:
- Draw their own villains or superheroes to place on the grid
- Draw or write their own instructions to use with the grid

SUPERMAN FACTS

 My real name is Kal-El.

 I come from a planet called Krypton.

 I left my planet when I was a baby because it was going to explode.

 I can fly and I can run and move faster than a bullet.

 I have x-ray vision which means I can see through walls.

 I have heat vision which means I can shoot heat from my eyes.

 I can freeze things with my first breath.

 I wear a blue and red costume to keep my true identity secret.

 Radioactive rocks called 'Kryptonite' are very dangerous to me because they weaken my powers and stop me moving.

 My arch enemy is Lex Luthor.

Challenge: **Super Mitts** Suggested Area of Provision: **Maths Area**

Enhance with:	Invite your children to:	Other possible enhancements:
- A selection of different sized gloves and mittens made of different materials - Superhero and villain labels to attach to each of the gloves - Items to fill the gloves e.g. small bricks, cubes, conkers, shells, big stones, marbles, ping pong balls etc - Number cards and number lines	Estimate how many objects will fit inside the different sized gloves and mittens. Encourage them to use their number skills to make sensible estimates and then check by counting.	- Socks, shoes or hats instead of gloves.

Select From the Following Suggested Focused Learning Possibilities

Communication & Language Listening & Attention	Physical Development Moving & Handling	Mathematics Numbers
Use this challenge to: Provide opportunities for your children to practise listening to and following a set of verbal instructions.	**Use this challenge to:** Provide opportunities for your children to develop their dexterity and fine motor skills.	**Use this challenge to:** Provide opportunities for your children to practise and apply the skills of counting and estimation.
I am learning to… - follow simple instructions (30-50) - concentrate until an activity is completed (40-60) - listen carefully and respond appropriately (ELG)	**I am learning to…** - hold small equipment with control (22-36) - use one handed tools (30-50) - handle equipment and tools with dexterity (ELG)	**I am learning to…** - talk about quantities (22-36) - count groups of objects (30-50) - estimate (40-60)
	Challenge your children to: Fill the gloves and mittens using tools such as pegs, tweezers etc instead of their fingers.	**Challenge your children to:** Solve problems by calculating how many objects would fit inside more than one mitten or glove by doubling the amounts e.g. if one glove holds 5, how many would 2 hold?

Characteristics of Effective Learning:

Engagement: I am learning to investigate
Motivation: I am learning to concentrate
Thinking: I am learning to talk about my thinking

Mark Making/Writing Opportunities

Invite your children to:
- Find a way of recording their estimates
- Write their calculations as number sentences

Enhancing Provision Through Superheroes

Challenge: **Super Talk**   Suggested Area of Provision: **Literacy Area**

Enhance with:	Invite your children to:	Other enhancements:
• A large picture frame filled with pictures of superhero and villain characters in different situations (comics are a useful resource) • Laminated speech bubbles • Whiteboard pens • Blue tac	Talk about what the characters are doing and what they might be saying. Encourage them to write words and sentences for the characters on the speech bubbles and attach them to the picture.	• Instead of using a picture frame cover a table top with the pictures.

Select From the Following Suggested Focused Learning Possibilities

Communication & Language — Speaking	Physical Development — Moving & Handling	Literacy — Writing
Use this challenge to: Provide opportunities for your children to practise rehearsing their ideas orally before writing.	**Use this challenge to:** Provide opportunities for your children to practise and develop their pencil control and tripod grip.	**Use this challenge to:** Provide opportunities for your children to practise recording their talk.
I am learning to… • talk in simple sentences (22-36) • use joining words in my talk (30-50) • keep to a topic when I talk (ELG)	**I am learning to…** • hold writing tools (22-36) • hold my pencil using a tripod grip (30-50) • form my letters correctly (40-60)	**I am learning to…** • comment on and explain some of the marks that I make (30-50) • use some correct letter shapes in my writing (40-60) • write simple sentences that I and others can read (ELG)
Challenge your children to: Create an oral narrative about what might be happening in the picture.	**Challenge your children to:** Keep their writing of a uniform size so that they can fit it into a speech bubble.	**Challenge your children to:** Use finger spaces and punctuation in their writing.

Characteristics of Effective Learning:

Engagement: I am learning to tackle things that may be difficult
Motivation: I am learning to be resilient when things get difficult
Thinking: I am learning to recognise when my previous learning or experiences link to what I am doing

Maths Opportunities for using vocabulary and applying skills

Invite your children to:
• Use prepositional language to describe where characters are in the picture.

Challenge: **Symmetrical Capes**　　　Suggested Area of Provision: **Maths Area**

Enhance with:	Invite your children to:	
• Laminated outlines of superhero capes with a line of symmetry down the middle. Some could also be divided into squares • Objects to place e.g. beads, counters, bottle tops, buttons, shapes etc • Mirrors • Key vocabulary e.g. prepositional language i.e. next to, beside, near, far, top, bottom, beside, before, after, opposite, between, below, above etc	Choose a cape and think carefully about how they can create a symmetrical pattern.	

Select From the Following Suggested Focused Learning Possibilities

Communication & Language Speaking	Mathematics Shape, Space & Measure	Expressive Arts & Design Exploring & Using Media & Materials
Use this challenge to: Provide opportunities for your children to narrate their ideas and thinking processes.	**Use this challenge to:** Provide opportunities for your children to notice, talk about and create their own patterns.	**Use this challenge to:** Provide opportunities for your children to develop and talk about their ideas by using resources in different ways.
I am learning to… • talk in simple sentences (22-36) • explain what is happening (30-50) • talk about my ideas (40-60)	**I am learning to…** • notice simple shapes and patterns (22-36) • use shape to create patterns (40-60) • make up my own patterns (ELG)	**I am learning to…** • experiment with some materials and media (22-36) • combine different media to create different effects (40-60) • experiment with a variety of materials to use in different ways (ELG)
Challenge your children to: Give reasons for their decisions and choices.	**Challenge your children to:** Mirror their pattern identically on each side of their cape.	**Challenge your children to:** Think of alternative ways to make a superhero cape.

Characteristics of Effective Learning:

Engagement: I am learning to use resources in unique and interesting ways
Motivation: I am learning to notice things in more detail
Thinking: I am learning to talk about how and what I am learning

Mark Making/Writing Opportunities

Invite your children to:
• Draw their own patterns

Challenge: **Super Character**   Suggested Area of Provision: **Creative Area**

Enhance with:	Invite your children to:
• Wooden spoons/spatulas • Lolly sticks • Dolly pegs • Corks • Card & paper of different colours & types • Pipe cleaners • Drawing materials • Collage materials • Googly eyes • Sequins • Pictures of superheroes & villains • Fixing and joining materials e.g. sellotape, glue, string, rubber bands	Create their own villain or superhero using either a wooden spoon, lolly stick, dolly peg or corks joined together as the body. Encourage them to add other materials as features, clothes, masks etc.

Select From the Following Suggested Focused Learning Possibilities

Physical Development Moving & Handling	Expressive Arts & Design Exploring & Using Media & Materials
Use this challenge to: Provide opportunities for your children to develop their dexterity and control over small apparatus and tools.	**Use this challenge to:** Provide opportunities for your children to explore how different materials can be used for different purposes to create different effects.
I am learning to… • use one-handed tools (30-50) • control and manipulate different tools safely (40-60) • handle equipment and writing tools with dexterity (ELG)	**I am learning to…** • experiment with some materials and media (22-36) • join pieces together to build (30-50) • combine different media to create different effects (40-60)
Challenge your children to: Use more challenging tools and equipment to create their character e.g. hole punch, split pins, stapler, paper clips etc.	**Challenge your children to:** Think of other ways to create a super character in both 2D and 3D representations.

Characteristics of Effective Learning:

Engagement: I am learning to use resources in unique and interesting ways
Motivation: I am learning to try different ways of doing things when one approach doesn't work
Thinking: I am learning to find different ways to do things

Mark Making/Writing Opportunities

Invite your children to…
- Draw or write a plan before they start.
- Draw and label the character they have made.

Challenge: **Super Tools**   Suggested Area of Provision: **Literacy Area**

Enhance with:	Invite your children to:	Other possible enhancements:
• A selection of objects wrapped in tin foil to create super tools that can be used for mark making e.g. canes, chopsticks, paintbrushes, knitting needles of different thicknesses, stirrers, spoons, forks, sticks, carrots, celery etc • Trays filled with desiccated coconut • Pictures of superhero logos	Choose a super tool and use it to draw a superhero logo. Encourage them to look carefully at the different shapes and practice anticlockwise movements and re-tracing over vertical lines. Suggest they find a way to record their pictures e.g. taking a photograph.	• Replace the logos with superhero words or pictures of superheroes and villains. • Colour the coconut by shaking it in a bag with a few drops of food colouring to match superhero colours e.g. red and blue. • Replace the coconut wit other substances e.g. shaving foam, flour, glitter, soil, icing sugar etc.

Select From the Following Suggested Focused Learning Possibilities

Physical Development Moving & Handling	Literacy Writing	
Use this challenge to: Provide opportunities for your children to practise and refine a tripod grip.	**Use this challenge to:** Provide opportunities for your children to practise forming lines and shapes to support correct letter formation.	
I am learning to… • copy simple shapes (22-36) • use one handed tools (30-50) • use anti-clockwise movements and retrace vertical lines (40-60)	**I am learning to…** • notice the difference between the marks that I make (22-36) • comment on and explain some of the marks that I make (30-50)	
Challenge your children to: Use writing tools in the trays e.g. pencils, felt-tips, pencil crayons, pens etc.	**Challenge your children to:** Replicate what they have done with their 'Super tools' using e.g. whiteboards and whiteboard pens, pieces of paper and felt-tips, chalks etc.	

Characteristics of Effective Learning:

Engagement: I am learning to investigate
Motivation: I am learning to notice things in more detail
Thinking: I am learning to talk about how and what I a learning

SUPER SHAPES INSTRUCTIONS

1. Choose your shapes.
2. Place them to make your superhero picture.
3. Draw round your shapes.
4. Cut out the shapes.
5. Stick the shapes to make your superhero picture.

Challenge: **Super Shapes**   Suggested Area of Provision: **Maths Area**

Enhance with:	Invite your children to:	Other possible enhancements:
• Scissors • Paper of different colours • 2D shapes • Pencils • Glue/sellotape/stapler • Instructions • Hole punch	Read and follow a set of instructions in order to create a superhero picture.	• Add rulers, compasses and protractors for children to create their own shapes instead of drawing around the shapes. • The children could use the shapes to print instead of drawing and cutting to create a superhero picture.

Select From the Following Suggested Focused Learning Possibilities

Communication & Language Speaking	Physical Development Moving & Handling	Mathematics Shape, Space & Measure
Use this challenge to: Provide opportunities for your children to practise narrating what they are doing, developing explanations and sequencing events.	**Use this challenge to:** Provide opportunities for your children to develop bi-lateral co-ordination (using 2 hands together) when using one handed tools e.g. scissors.	**Use this challenge to:** Provide opportunities for your children to name, describe and talk about shapes.
I am learning to… • talk in simple sentences (22-36) • explain what is happening (30-50) • talk about events in sequence (40-60)	**I am learning to…** • use one-handed tools (30-50) • control and manipulate different tools safely (40-60) • handle equipment and tools with dexterity (ELG)	**I am learning to…** • use shapes appropriately in my play (30-50) • use mathematical words to describe shapes (40-60) • describe objects and shapes using mathematical vocabulary (ELG)
Challenge your children to: Provide more detail in their explanations.	**Challenge your children to:** Join their shapes together using more challenging tools such as staplers, hole punches, split pins etc.	**Challenge your children to:** Use irregular shapes to create their superhero picture.

Characteristics of Effective Learning:

Engagement: I am learning that when I practise things I can get better
Motivation: I am learning to persist even when things get difficult
Thinking: I am learning to plan

Mark Making/Writing Opportunities

Invite your children to:
- Label their picture
- Write their own set of instructions

SUPER POEM

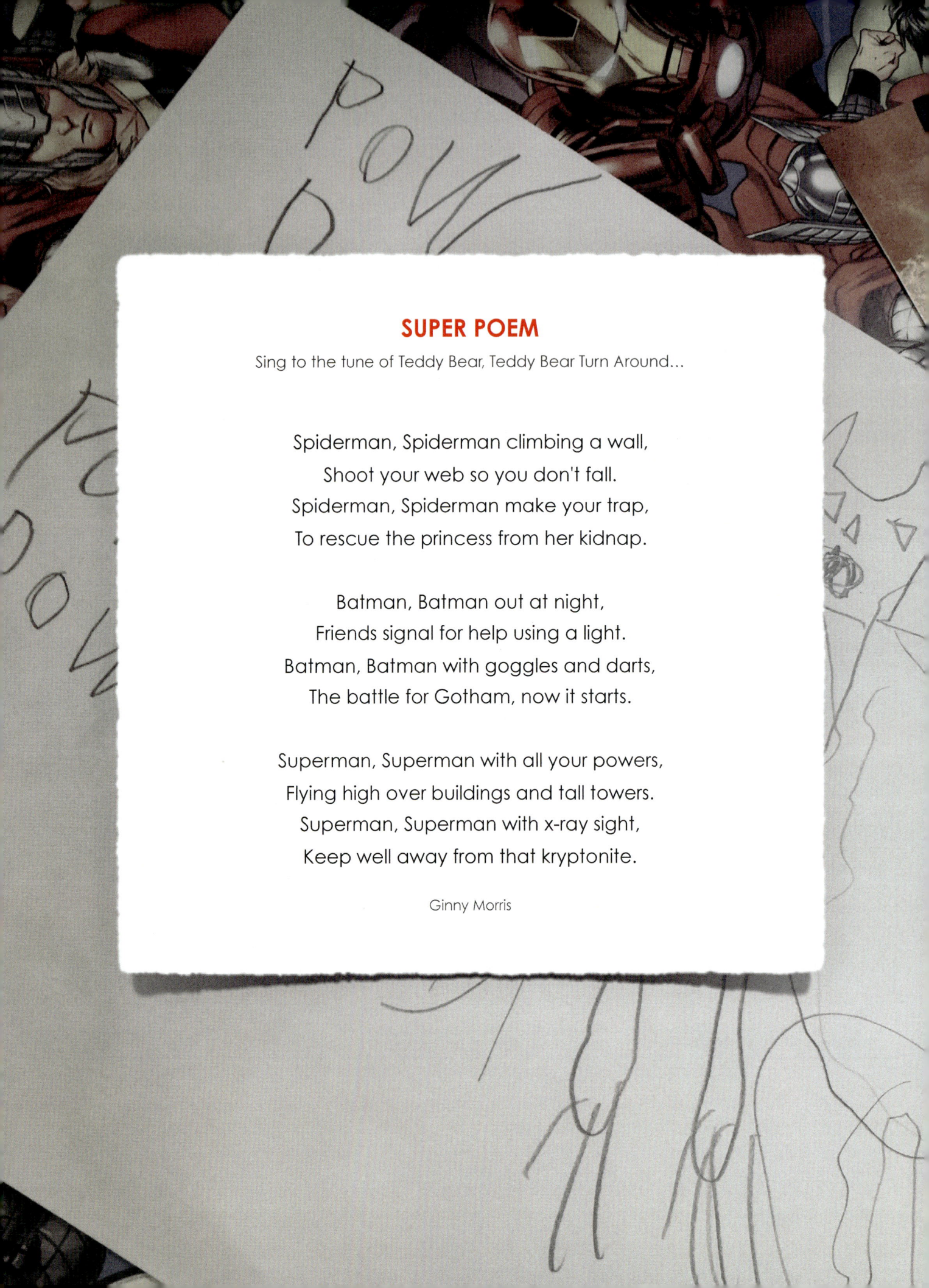

Sing to the tune of Teddy Bear, Teddy Bear Turn Around...

Spiderman, Spiderman climbing a wall,
Shoot your web so you don't fall.
Spiderman, Spiderman make your trap,
To rescue the princess from her kidnap.

Batman, Batman out at night,
Friends signal for help using a light.
Batman, Batman with goggles and darts,
The battle for Gotham, now it starts.

Superman, Superman with all your powers,
Flying high over buildings and tall towers.
Superman, Superman with x-ray sight,
Keep well away from that kryptonite.

Ginny Morris

Challenge: **Super Touch** Suggested Area of Provision: **Investigation Area**

Enhance with:	Invite your children to:	Other possible enhancements:
• Balloons filled with different substances e.g. dried peas, sand, honey, rice, water, baby lotion, uncooked pasta, cotton wool, dried fruit etc. Hang them from a washing line or lay them out on a table • Clipboards to record their observations • Descriptive vocabulary e.g. hard, soft, lumpy, bumpy, smooth, spiky, jagged, squashy etc	Feel the different balloons and use their hands to investigate what might be inside the balloons. Encourage them to make predictions and talk about and describe what they can feel and what they think might be inside.	• Replace the balloons with superhero rubber gloves.

Select From the Following Suggested Focused Learning Possibilities

Personal, Social & Emotional Development Self-confidence & Self-awareness	Communication & Language Speaking	Understanding the World The World
Use this challenge to: Provide opportunities for your children to practise making independent choices and decisions and talk about their reasons.	**Use this challenge to:** Provide opportunities for your children to learn and use new vocabulary.	**Use this challenge to:** Provide opportunities for your children to explore and talk about similarities and differences and properties of materials.
I am learning to… • choose activities and resources with help (30-50) • talk to other people about what I am interested in (40-60) • say why I like some activities more than others (ELG)	**I am learning to…** • use new words in my talking (22-36) • use new words that reflect my experiences (30-50) • use and explore new vocabulary (40-60)	**I am learning to…** • talk about some of the things I have noticed in the world around me (30-50) • notice and talk about how some things are the same and some are different (40-60) • notice and talk about similarities ad differences between materials (ELG)
Challenge your children to: Talk about what they are good at what they find more difficult.	**Challenge your children to:** Make comparisons using their descriptive vocabulary e.g. "It feels as prickly as a hedgehog."	**Challenge your children to:** Describe the properties of different materials e.g. strong, weak, flexible, hard, soft, shiny, waterproof etc.

Characteristics of Effective Learning:

Engagement: I am learning to investigate
Motivation: I am learning to choose the things that really fascinate me
Thinking: I am learning to predict

Mark Making/Writing Opportunities

Invite your children to:
• Label the balloons with their ideas of what might be inside.

Challenge: **Super Words**   Suggested Area of Provision: **Literacy Area**

Enhance with:	Invite your children to:	Other possible enhancements:
• Small jars labelled with either superhero or villain labels and pictures • Counters • Whiteboards • Whiteboard pens • Superhero flashcards with words e.g. Pow, Zap, Pop, Bang etc	Play a game in pairs. Who can fill their jar with superpowers first? Suggest they decide which jar they are going to fill.. They should each take a whiteboard and pen and decide from the flashcards which word to put in the centre of their boards first. The aim of the game is to copy the word into each of the 4 corners of their board. The winner is the first person to write the word in each corner correctly. They then put one token superpower in their jar. Who can fill their jar first?	• Flashcards with include individual letter shapes, children's names or tricky words instead of superhero words.

Select From the Following Suggested Focused Learning Possibilities

Personal, Social & Emotional Development Managing Feelings & Behaviour	Literacy Reading	Literacy Writing
Use this challenge to: Provide opportunities for your children to work together to make decisions and choices.	**Use this challenge to:** Provide opportunities for your children to use and apply their phonic skills.	**Use this challenge to:** Provide opportunities for your children to become more fluent in their writing.
I am learning to… • co-operate with some boundaries and routines (22-36) • take turns and share with support (30-50) • work as part of a group (ELG)	**I am learning to…** • recognise familiar words (30-50) • segment sounds in simple words and blend them together (40-60) • use my phonic knowledge to read regular words our loud (ELG)	**I am learning to…** • write labels, captions (40-60) • spell words phonetically in my writing (ELG) • write irregular common words (ELG)
Challenge your children to: Listen to others to help think of new ways to play the game with different rules.	**Challenge your children to:** Use their phonic skills to help them read more complex words.	**Challenge your children to:** Look at the word before they start writing and then remove it so that they have to write it from memory.

Characteristics of Effective Learning:

Engagement: I am learning that when I practise things I can get better
Motivation: I am learning to be resilient when things get difficult
Motivation: I am learning to talk about when I feel proud

Maths Opportunities for using vocabulary and applying skills

Invite your children to:
• Calculate the value of the jars if each token is worth e.g. 2 points / 10 points etc.
• Compare and count the amount of counters in the jars.

BATMAN FACTS

   My real name is Bruce Wayne.

   I live in a place called Gotham City.

   I work hard to protect everyone who lives there.

   I drive a car called a 'Batmobile'.

   I use special tools which I keep in a 'utility' belt.

   One of my tools is a 'Batarang' which is a boomerang shaped like a bat.

   I have help from my friends Robin, Alfred and Commissioner Gordon to keep Gotham City safe.

   Commissioner Gordon uses the Bat Symbol to tell me he needs help. It is a light in the sky in the shape of a bat.

   I wear a grey and black costume and my cape can spread out into wings so I can glide down safely from high buildings.

   My enemies are Joker, Penguin, Cat Woman and Mr Freeze.

Challenge: **Measuring Sticks** Suggested Area of Provision: **Outdoors**

Enhance with:	Invite your children to:	Other possible enhancements:
• Garden canes of different lengths with pictures of superhero characters stuck to one end • A list or pictures of suggested objects to measure e.g. fence, adult, wheeled vehicle, tree, wall, table etc • Key mathematical vocabulary e.g. length, longer, shorter, taller, higher, smaller etc • Clipboards to record measurements	Choose a Superhero Measuring Stick and find out which objects are taller, shorter, or the same height as their Superhero Measuring Stick.	• Instead of a list of objects use photographs and names of the children to encourage them to measure each other against the Superhero Measuring Sticks.

Select From the Following Suggested Focused Learning Possibilities

Communication & Language Understanding	Communication & Language Speaking	Mathematics Shape, Space & Measure
Use this challenge to: Provide opportunities for your children to understand and follow verbal instructions.	**Use this challenge to:** Provide opportunities for your children to talk about what they are doing, their thinking processes and their ideas.	**Use this challenge to:** Provide opportunities for your children to compare, order, measure and talk about height.
I am learning to… • follow a simple one part instruction (30-50) • follow a 2 part instruction (40-60) • follow more complex instructions that involve several ideas or actions (ELG)	**I am learning to…** • explain what is happening (30-50) • talk clearly about what I am thinking (40-60) • describe and explain my ideas (ELG)	**I am learning to…** • use the language of size (22-36) • order objects by height (40-60) • use the correct vocabulary to talk about size (ELG)
	Challenge your children to: Give reasons for their thinking.	**Challenge your children to:** Use standard measures to check the height of the objects they have measured with their measuring sticks.

Characteristics of Effective Learning:

Engagement: I am learning to find out more about something
Motivation: I am learning to notice things in more details
Thinking: I am learning to set hypotheses and test out my ideas

Mark Making/Writing Opportunities

Invite your children to:
- Record the results of their measuring in pictures and /or words.
- Draw or write additional labels to create new Superhero Measuring Sticks.

Challenge: **Metal Man**   Suggested Area of Provision: **Investigation**

Enhance with:	Invite your children to:	Other possible enhancements:
• Small shallow trays of water filled with a selection of objects which are magnetic and non-magnetic e.g. washers, screws, bolts, silver and plastic bottle tops, coins, paper clips, spoons, metal and plastic buttons, split pins, keys, grips, springs, dice, lego etc • Magnets • Plastic trays for children to use for placing • Pictures of Metal Man	Come to the rescue of Metal Man who has been destroyed by a villain leaving all his parts in the water. Explain to the children that they need to use the magnets to find out which of the objects in the water tray belong to the Metal Man. Encourage them to use the magnets to collect the magnetic objects and to then place the objects to recreate Metal Man.	

Select From the Following Suggested Focused Learning Possibilities

Communication & Language Speaking	Understanding the World The World	Expressive Arts & Design Exploring & Using Media & Materials
Use this challenge to: Provide opportunities for your children to learn and use new vocabulary developing their explanations.	**Use this challenge to:** Provide opportunities for your children to be curious and ask questions to extend their knowledge.	**Use this challenge to:** Provide opportunities for your children to explore different ways of using resources to express their ideas.
I am learning to… • use new words in my talking (22-36) • explain what is happening (30-50) • talk about my ideas (40-60)	**I am learning to…** • talk about why things happen (30-50) • talk about similarities and differences between materials (40-60) • notice and talk about how some things are the same and some are different (ELG)	**I am learning to…** • experiment with some materials and media (22-36) • change my work when I need to (40-60) • experiment with a variety of materials to use in different ways (ELG)
Challenge your children to: Give detailed explanations about what they have discovered about magnets.	**Challenge your children to:** Find other materials that are magnetic.	**Challenge your children to:** Think of other characters that they could create based on the properties of materials.

Characteristics of Effective Learning:

Engagement: I am learning to find out more about something
Motivation: I am learning to concentrate
Thinking: I am learning to set hypotheses and test out my ideas

Mark Making/Writing Opportunities

Invite your children to:
• Draw a representation of their metal man.

Maths Opportunities for using vocabulary and applying skills

Invite your children to:
• Talk about the names and properties of the shapes of the objects that they use.

Enhancing Provision Through Superheroes

Challenge: **Super Scene**   Suggested Area of Provision: **Construction & Small World**

Enhance with:	Invite your children to:	Other possible enhancements:
• Bricks covered in black paper and yellow stickers/paper for windows, to represent buildings at night • Shallow trays filled with different materials to represent hazards e.g red, orange and yellow tissue paper for fire, masking tape to create a spider web, green sponge cut up for kryptonite • Key themed words e.g. help, rescue, muscles, mask, cape, disguise, rescue, climb, fast, flying, villain, breathe fire, breathe ice • Small world figures	Create their own narratives using the scene and props. Encourage the children to talk about their ideas and to put a sequence of events together to create their own oral story.	• Create on a larger scale outside with large cardboard boxes, tuff spots and water trays. • Children could create their own version of a superhero scene using smaller resources e.g. matchboxes for the buildings, yoghurt pots and plastic pots for the hazards.

Select From the Following Suggested Focused Learning Possibilities

Personal, Social & Emotional Development Making Relationships	Communication & Language Speaking	Expressive Arts & Design Being Imaginative
Use this challenge to: Provide opportunities for your children to develop their co-operation as they play alongside other children talking about and sharing their ideas.	Use this challenge to: Provide opportunities for your children to practise oral story telling.	Use this challenge to: Provide opportunities for your children to develop their imagination.
I am learning to… • join in with others during my play (22-36) • play in a group (30-50) • play co-operatively (ELG)	I am learning to… • talk in simple sentences (22-36) • retell something that has happened in the right order (30-50) • tell stories orally (40-60)	I am learning to… • play imaginatively by pretending (22-36) • tell my own simple story using toys (30-50) • create a storyline in my play (40-60)
Challenge your children to: Listen to and take account of others' ideas.	Challenge your children to: • Add descriptive detail to their oral narrative. • Use time words to sequence their story e.g. first, next, in the beginning, finally.	Challenge your children to: Choose and add different ways to represent their ideas and thoughts.

Characteristics of Effective Learning:

Engagement: I am learning to pretend that objects are something else
Motivation: I am learning to choose the things that really fascinate me
Thinking: I am learning to think of my own ideas

Mark Making/Writing Opportunities

Invite your children to:
• Find a way to record their stories.

Maths Opportunities for using vocabulary and applying skills

Invite your children to:
• Use prepositional language in their narratives.

Challenge: **Elastic Man**   Suggested Area of Provision: **Finger Gym**

Enhance with:	Invite your children to:
• Geo boards • Elastic bands of different thicknesses, lengths and colours • Pictures of Elastic Man	Experiment with attaching the elastic bands to the board to create an outline of Elastic Man. Suggest that they think about what shapes they can make on the board to form different parts of his body e.g. a triangle head, a square body, long rectangular arms.

Select From the Following Suggested Focused Learning Possibilities

Physical Development Moving & Handling	Mathematics Shape, Space & Measure
Use this challenge to: Provide opportunities for your children to develop their fine motor skills.	**Use this challenge to:** Provide opportunities for your children to investigate and talk about shapes and their properties using the correct mathematical vocabulary.
I am learning to… • hold small equipment with control (22-36) • control and manipulate different tools safely (40-60) • handle equipment with dexterity (ELG)	**I am learning to…** • notice simple shapes and patterns (22-36) • use shapes appropriately in my play (30-50) • use the correct names for 2D shapes (40-60)
	Challenge your children to: • Talk about the properties of the shapes they are creating • Create irregular shapes using the elastic bands.

Characteristics of Effective Learning:

Engagement: I am learning to use resources in unique and interesting ways

Motivation: I am learning to persist even when things get difficult

Thinking: I am learning to talk about the problems I encounter and find ways to solve them

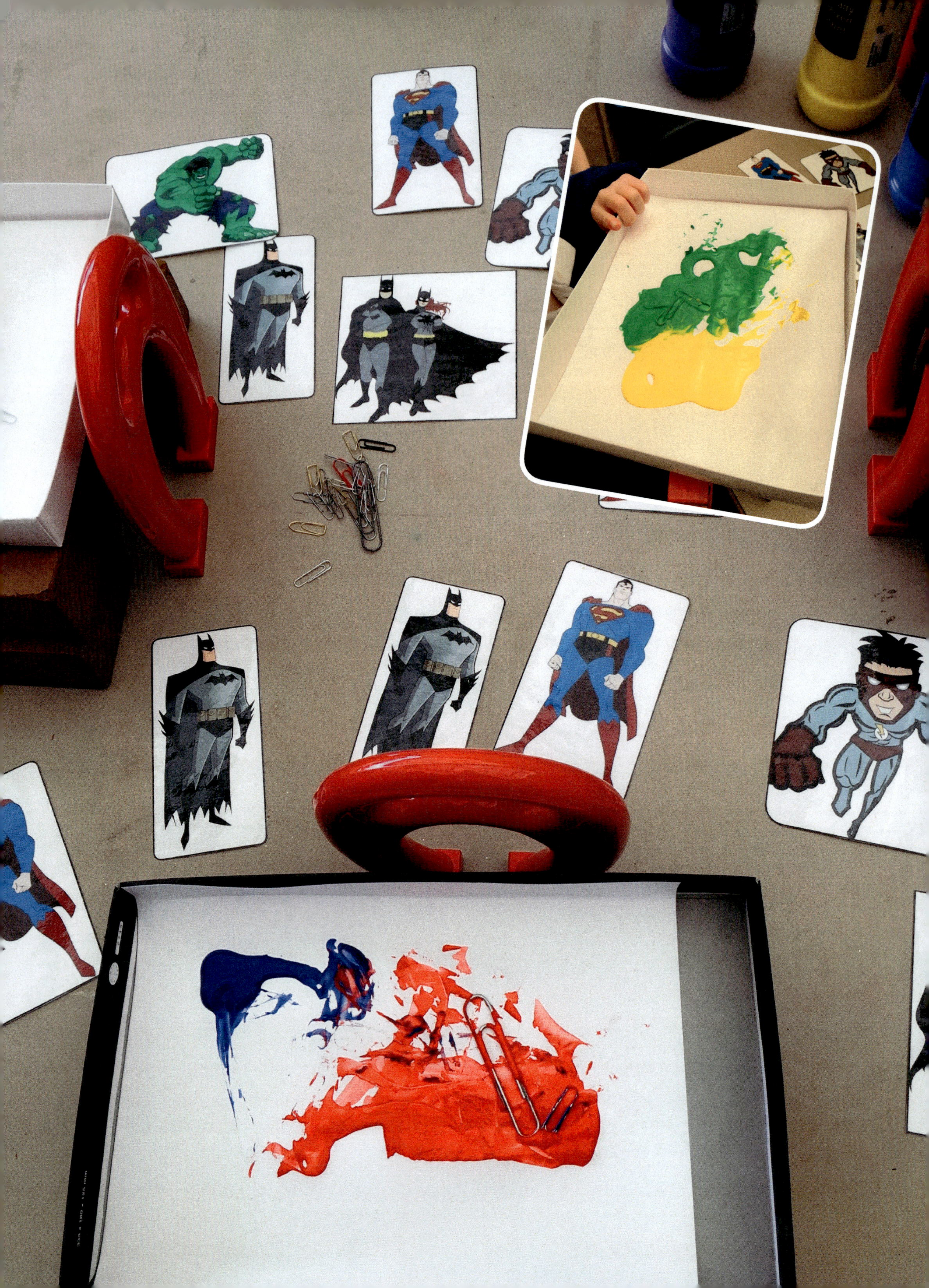

Challenge: **Super Strong** Suggested Area of Provision: **Creative Area**

Enhance with:	Invite your children to:	Other possible enhancements:
• Shallow boxes e.g. lids from boxes lined with a piece of paper • Small plastic squeezy bottles filled with different coloured paint • Paper clips • Strong magnets • Pictures of superheroes & villains	Choose their favourite superhero character and think about the colours that are associated with their choice. Suggest they squeeze small dots of their chosen coloured paint onto the paper. Encourage them to add a paper clip to the paint and then use a magnet underneath the box to move the paperclip around the paper to create different patterns.	• Instead of a paperclip use other metal objects e.g. metal car, screws, keys, grips, coins. • Mix paint with other substances e.g. sand, glitter, rice to create a different effect.

Select From the Following Suggested Focused Learning Possibilities

Physical Development Moving & Handling	Expressive Arts & Design Exploring & Using Media & Materials	Understanding the World The World
Use this challenge to: Provide opportunities for your children to develop their bi-lateral co-ordination (using two hands together).	**Use this challenge to:** Provide opportunities for your children to explore how different materials can create different effects.	**Use this challenge to:** Provide opportunities for your children to explore the properties of magnets.
I am learning to… • hold small equipment with control (22-36) • use simple tools to change materials (40-60) • control and co-ordinate my large and small movements (ELG)	**I am learning to…** • experiment with some materials and media (22-36) • explore colours to see how they can be changed (30-50) • explore colours by mixing (40-60)	**I am learning to…** • talk about how things happen (30-50) • look closely and notice patterns (40-60) • notice and talk about similarities and differences between materials (ELG)
Challenge your children to: Hold the box in one hand and the magnet in the other.		**Challenge your children to:** Describe the properties of magnets e.g. they attract some metal, some are very strong, some objects stick to magnets and some don't.

Characteristics of Effective Learning:

Engagement: I am learning to investigate
Motivation: I am learning to concentrate
Thinking: I am learning to talk about my thinking

Maths Opportunities for using vocabulary and applying skills

Invite your children to:
• Notice and talk about the shapes and patterns that they see.

Enhancing Provision Through Superheroes

SPIDERMAN FACTS

- I have super strength and can climb up most things including tall buildings.

- I have a 'spider sense' that lets me know if my enemies are near.

- I can shoot webs from my wrist to trap animals and grab things.

- I can swing from building to building using my web.

- When I was a boy I was bitten by a radioactive spider and that is how I got my superpowers.

- I use my special powers to protect the people who live in New York.

- My real name is Peter Parker.

- My enemies are Green Goblin, Dr Octopus and The Scorpion.

- When I am not Spiderman I work for a newspaper, the Daily Bugle, selling pictures of myself as Spiderman.

- I live with my Aunt May.

Challenge: **Baddie Traps**   Suggested Area of Provision: **Construction Area**

Enhance with:	Invite your children to:	Other possible enhancements:
• Lolly sticks • Cardboard tubes and boxes • Small world figures • Thick string • Thick pieces of card • Wire cooling trays • Pegs • Straws • Cotton reels • Material • CD's	Design and build a trap to catch villains or baddies. Encourage them to plan their design first and then carefully choose the resources they will need.	• Metal colanders and sieves.

Select From the Following Suggested Focused Learning Possibilities

Communication & Language Speaking	Expressive Arts & Design Being Imaginative
Use this challenge to: Provide opportunities for your children to explain and describe their ideas and thinking processes.	**Use this challenge to:** Provide opportunities for your children to explore different ways of using resources to express their ideas.
I am learning to… • explain what is happening (30-50) • talk clearly about what I am thinking (40-60) • describe and explain events and my ideas (ELG)	**I am learning to…** • play imaginatively by pretending (22-36) • create props for my role play (30-50) • play co-operatively with others to act out a narrative (40-60)
Challenge your children to: Provide reasons for their decisions and choices.	**Challenge your children to:** Look at each other's designs and creations and give feedback about what they think is good and why.

Characteristics of Effective Learning:

Engagement: I am learning to use resources in unique and interesting ways
Motivation: I am learning to try different ways of doing things when one approach doesn't work
Thinking: I am learning to set hypotheses and test out my ideas

Mark Making/Writing Opportunities

Invite your children to:
• Draw or write a plan before they make their trap.

Maths Opportunities for using vocabulary and applying skills

Invite your children to:
• Use positional language to describe how they put their resources together.

Enhancing Provision Through Superheroes

EXCITING EXPLOSIONS

INSTRUCTIONS

1. Fill the pot half full with vinegar.
2. Stir in 1 spoonful of paint.
3. Add a big squeeze of washing up liquid.
4. Add lots of glitter!
5. Add 1 spoonful of bicarbonate of soda.
6. Stir together.
7. Watch what happens.

Challenge: **Exciting Explosions**		Suggested Area of Provision: **Investigation Area**
Enhance with:	**Invite your children to:**	**Other possible enhancements:**
• Bicarbonate of soda • Vinegar • Washing up liquid • Powder Paint • Glitter • Sequins • Small plastic pots • A super stirrer (cover a spoon or chopstick with foil) • Sets of instructions	Make their own exciting explosion by following the instructions. Encourage them to follow the correct sequence and to look closely at what happens.	

Select From the Following Suggested Focused Learning Possibilities

Communication & Language **Speaking**	**Literacy** **Reading**	**Understanding the World** **The World**
Use this challenge to: Provide opportunities for your children to develop talk by extending vocabulary, developing sentence structure and putting their thoughts into words.	**Use this challenge to:** Provide opportunities for your children to practise and apply their phonic knowledge to help them read simple words and sentences.	**Use this challenge to:** Provide opportunities for your children to carry out simple experiments, looking closely at what happens and talking about what they notice.
I am learning to… • talk in simple sentences (22-36) • explain what is happening (30-50) • use and explore new vocabulary (40-60)	**I am learning to…** • recognise familiar words and signs (30-50) • read simple words and sentences (40-60) • read and understand simple sentences (ELG)	**I am learning to…** • talk about why things happen (30-50) • look closely and notice changes that take place over time (40-60) • answer 'why' and 'how' questions (ELG)
Challenge your children to: Use more descriptive vocabulary to describe what is happening.	**Challenge your children to:** Read irregular high frequency words and words of more than one syllable.	

Characteristics of Effective Learning:

Engagement: I am learning to investigate
Motivation: I am learning to choose the things that really fascinate me
Thinking: I am learning to talk about my thinking

Maths Opportunities for using vocabulary and applying skills

Invite your children to:
• Count out the correct spoonfuls of ingredients.

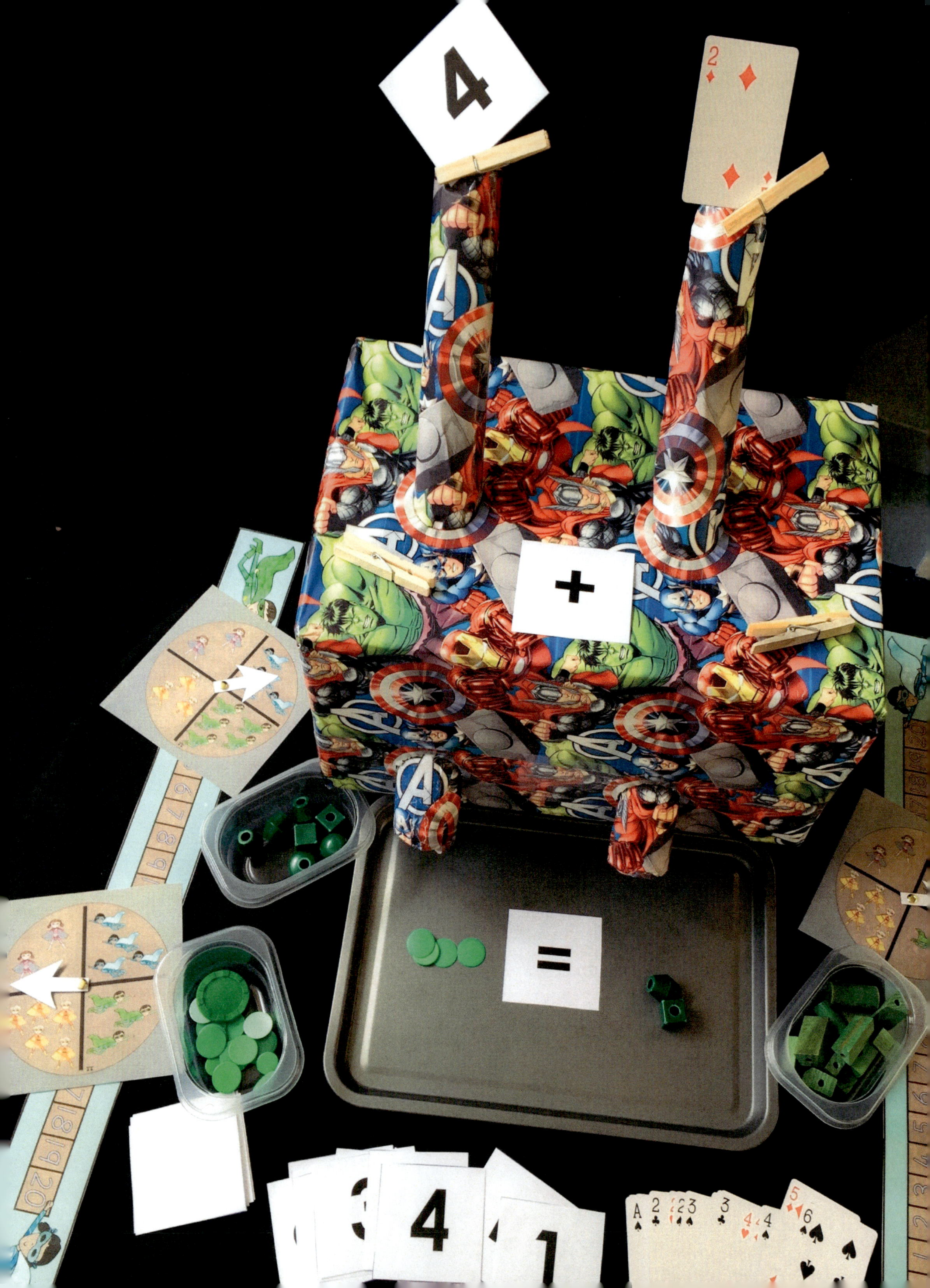
4
+
=
4
1

Challenge: **Kryptonite Calculations**　　　　　　　　　　Suggested Area of Provision: **Maths Area**

Enhance with:	Invite your children to:	Other possible enhancements:
- A large box covered with superhero wrapping paper. Cut 2 holes in the top and 2 holes in the side and put a cardboard tube through both holes. Attach a peg to the top of the tubes and a tray at the bottom to catch the counters - Number cards - Number lines and spinners - Addition signs - Green counters - Whiteboards and pens	Use the spinners to decide which two number cards to attach to the pegs at the top of each tube. Place an addition sign in the middle. Encourage them to collect the right amount of counters for each tube and then post them down the tubes into the collecting tray. Encourage them to count the total number of objects in the tray to find the answer. They could then use the number cards to create a number sentence or write it on the whiteboard.	- Insert only one tube so children can practise counting out objects to match the number pegged on the tube.

Select From the Following Suggested Focused Learning Possibilities

Personal, Social & Emotional Development Self-confidence & Self-awareness	Communication & Language Understanding	Mathematics Numbers
Use this challenge to: Provide opportunities for your children to develop their independence and confidence to tackle challenges and talk about how they get on.	**Use this challenge to:** Provide opportunities for your children to practise listening to, processing and carrying out instructions.	**Use this challenge to:** Provide opportunities for your children to become more fluent in their number skills.
I am learning to… - ask for help (30-50) - talk about what I can do (40-60) - decide for myself when I do and do not need help (ELG)	**I am learning to…** - follow a simple one part instruction (30-50) - follow a 2 part instruction (40-60) - follow more complex instructions (ELG)	**I am learning to…** - match numerals with an amount of objects (30-50) - count two groups of objects together to find the total (40-60) - add together 2 single digit numbers (ELG)
Challenge your children to: Ask each other for help and support in tackling challenges.	**Challenge your children to:** Follow a set of verbal instructions in sequence e.g. First choose a number for your answer. Next think about how many ways you could make this answer. Finally think of a way to record your ideas.	**Challenge your children to:** Tackle calculations using larger numbers.

Characteristics of Effective Learning:

Engagement: I am learning to tackle things that may be difficult
Motivation: I am learning to be resilient when things get difficult
Thinking: I am learning to talk about the problems I encounter and find ways to solve them

Mark Making/Writing Opportunities

Invite your children to:
- Record their calculations.

MR STICKY

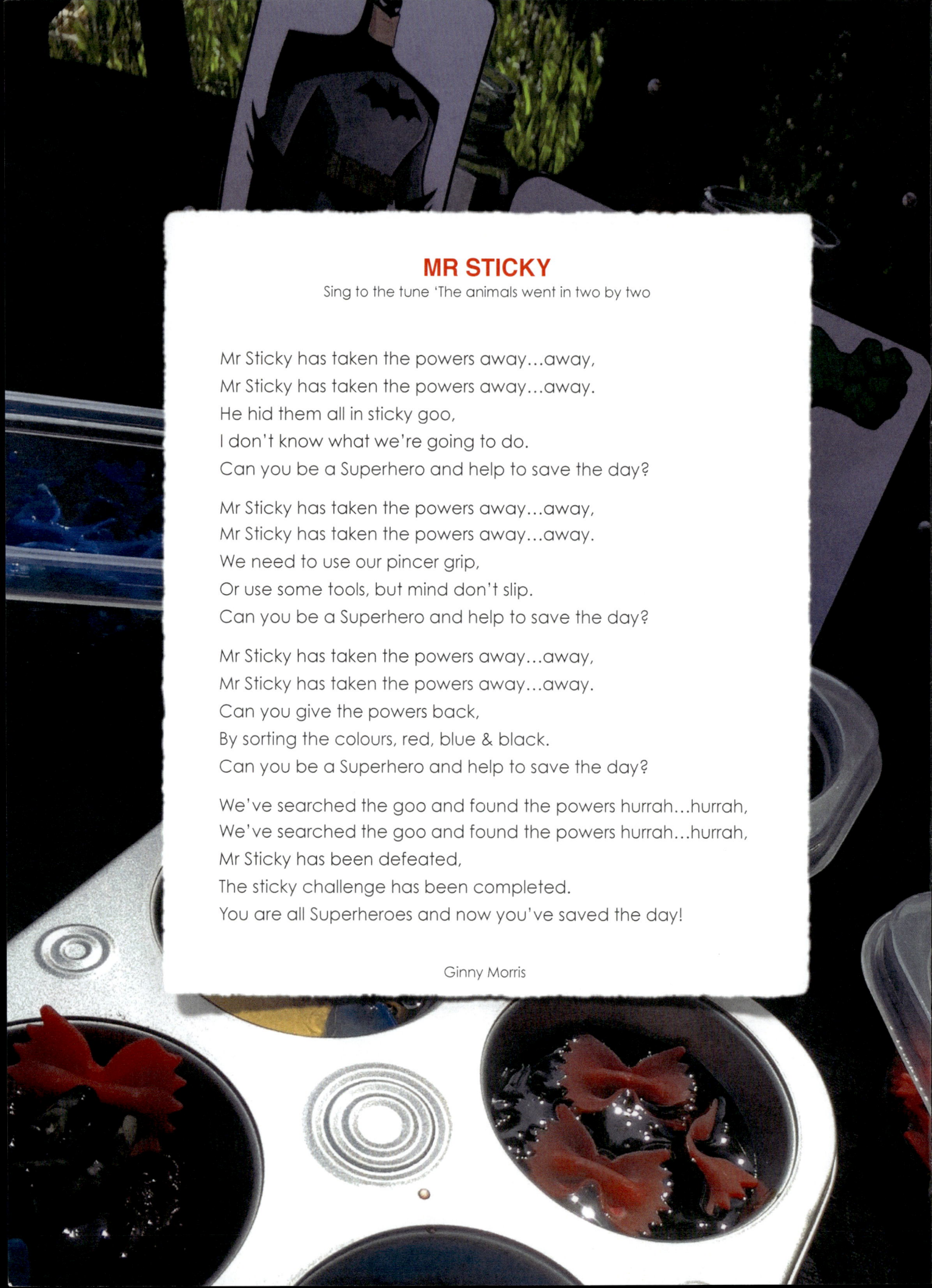

Sing to the tune 'The animals went in two by two

Mr Sticky has taken the powers away…away,
Mr Sticky has taken the powers away…away.
He hid them all in sticky goo,
I don't know what we're going to do.
Can you be a Superhero and help to save the day?

Mr Sticky has taken the powers away…away,
Mr Sticky has taken the powers away…away.
We need to use our pincer grip,
Or use some tools, but mind don't slip.
Can you be a Superhero and help to save the day?

Mr Sticky has taken the powers away…away,
Mr Sticky has taken the powers away…away.
Can you give the powers back,
By sorting the colours, red, blue & black.
Can you be a Superhero and help to save the day?

We've searched the goo and found the powers hurrah…hurrah,
We've searched the goo and found the powers hurrah…hurrah,
Mr Sticky has been defeated,
The sticky challenge has been completed.
You are all Superheroes and now you've saved the day!

Ginny Morris

Challenge: **Mr Sticky**   Suggested Area of Provision: **Investigation Area**

Enhance with:	Invite your children to:
• Muffin trays filled with different sticky substances e.g. treacle, honey, golden syrup, melted marshmallows, marmalade, jam, marmite etc • Coloured pasta of different shapes and sizes • Small bowls/jars labelled with Superheroes pictures • Timers • Tools e.g. pegs, tweezers, tongs etc	Come to the rescue of the Superheroes who have had their superpowers stolen by Mr Sticky. Encourage them to think about the best way to remove the pasta (the superpowers) from the sticky substances. Tell the children that there is a time limit and they need to collect as many superpowers as they can before the timer runs out.

Select From the Following Suggested Focused Learning Possibilities

Communication & Language Speaking	Physical Development Moving & Handling	Understanding the World The World
Use this challenge to: Provide opportunities for your children to build up their vocabulary by learning and using new descriptive words.	Use this challenge to: Provide opportunities for your children to develop their pincer grip and fine motor dexterity.	Use this challenge to: Provide opportunities for your children to investigate using their senses.
I am learning to… • use new words in my talking (22-36) • use new words that reflect my experiences (30-50) • use and explore new vocabulary (40-60)	I am learning to… • to hold small equipment with control (22-36) • control and manipulate different tools safely (40-60) • handle equipment and tools with dexterity (ELG)	I am learning to… • talk about some of the things I have noticed (30-50) • look closely and notice how some things are different and some are the same (40-60) • notice and talk about similarities and differences between materials (ELG)
Challenge your children to: Describe and explain what they doing in more detail.		Challenge your children to: Describe the properties of the different materials they are using e.g. strong, weak, flexible, hard, soft, shiny, runny etc.

Characteristics of Effective Learning:

Engagement: I am learning to investigate
Motivation: I am learning to persist even when things get difficult
Thinking: I am learning to find different ways to do things

Maths Opportunities for using vocabulary and applying skills

Invite your children to:
• Count and record how many superpowers they have rescued

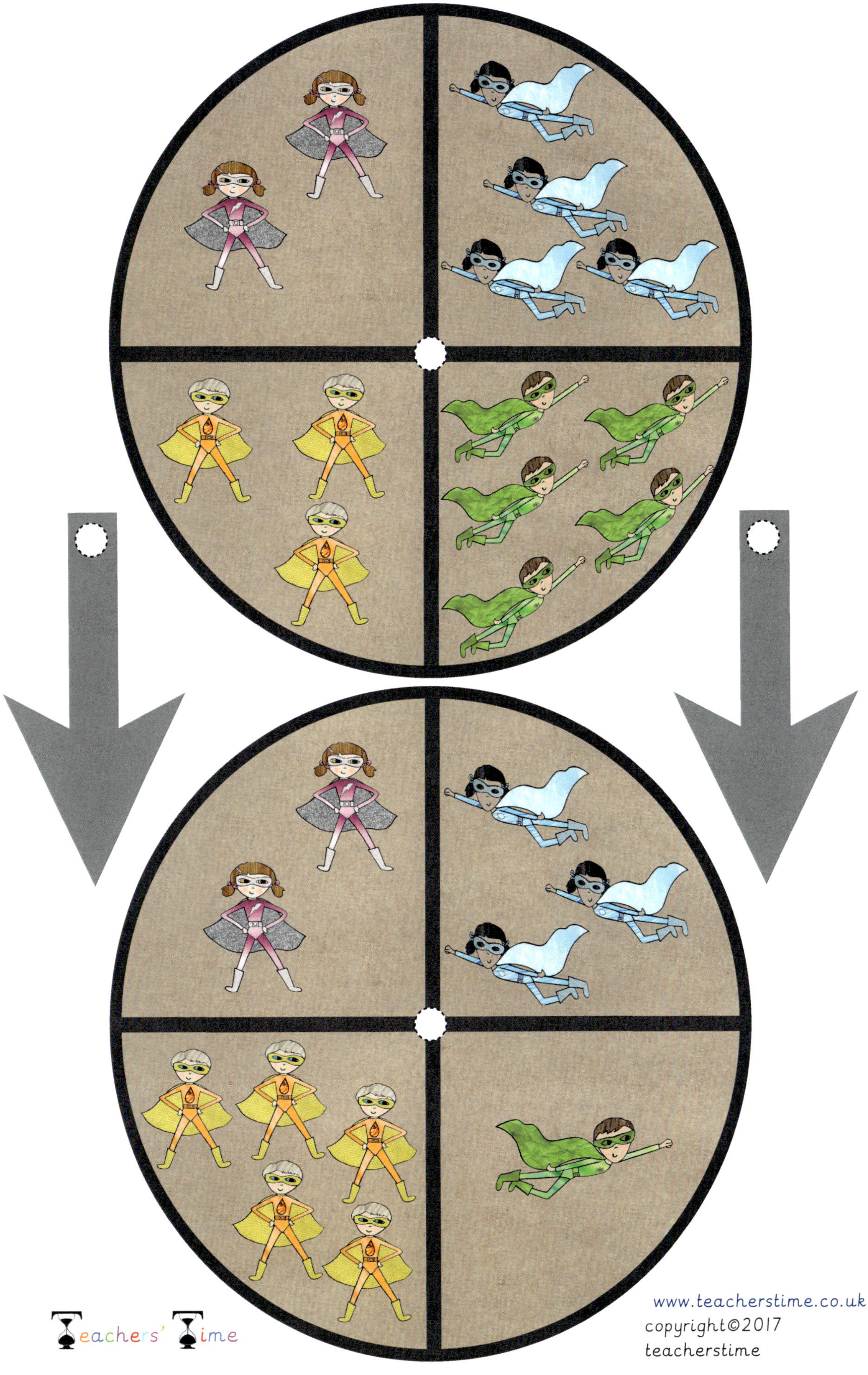

Teachers' Time

www.teacherstime.co.uk

Other Books
by Nicky Simmons and Ginny Morris

Learning In Early Years Series

Available Now….

Enhancing Provision Through Minibeasts (ISBN 1537458418)

Enhancing Provision Through Space (ISBN 1542316682)

Enhancing Provision Through Dinosaurs (ISBN 1544161495)

Enhancing Provision Through Superheroes (this book)

Available Soon…

Enhancing Provision Through Under the Sea

Enhancing Provision Through Monsters

Enhancing Provision Through Traditional Tales

Enhancing Provision Through Nursery Rhymes

Enhancing Provision Through Growing

Other Publications

Planning for Learning in Early Years (ISBN 1530228010)

Made in the USA
Columbia, SC
15 May 2017